Fact Finders®

MUDSKIPPERS

AND OTHER *EXTREME* FISH ADAPTATIONS

by Jody Sullivan Rake

Consultant:
Robert T. Mason
Professor of Integrative Biology
Oregon State University
Corvallis, Oregon

CAPSTONE PRESS
a capstone imprint

Fact Finders Books are published by Capstone Press,
1710 Roe Crest Drive, North Mankato, Minnesota 56003
www.capstonepub.com

Library of Congress Cataloging-in-Publication Data
Rake, Jody Sullivan, author.
  Mudskippers and other extreme fish adaptations / by Jody Sullivan Rake.
    pages cm. — (Fact finders. Extreme adaptations)
  Summary: "Explores various extreme fish adaptations throughout the world, including wrasses, anglerfish, and grunions"—Provided by publisher.
  Audience: Ages 8-10.
  Audience: Grades 4 to 6.
  Includes bibliographical references and index.
  ISBN 978-1-4914-0165-1 (library binding)
  ISBN 978-1-4914-0170-5 (paperback)
  ISBN 978-1-4914-0174-3 (eBook pdf)
1. Fishes—Adaptation—Juvenile literature. 2. Adaptation (Biology)—Juvenile literature. I. Title.
  QL617.2.R35 2015
  597.14—dc23   2014006948

Developed and Produced by Focus Strategic Communications, Inc.
  Adrianna Edwards: project manager
  Ron Edwards, Jessica Pegis: editors
  Rob Scanlan: designer and compositor
  Diane Hartmann: media researcher
  Francine Geraci: copy editor and proofreader
  Wendy Scavuzzo: fact checker

Photo Credits
Alamy: Steve Bloom Images, 25; Dreamstime: Michael Klenetsky, 10, Nozyer, 6; iStock: Dorling Kindersley, 5; National Oceanography Centre, UK/R.Lampitt, 20; Nature Picture Library: David Shale, 24, Doug Perrine, 11, 21, Jane Burton, 28, Kim Taylor, 7; Shutterstock: bikeriderlondon, 8, BOONCHUAY PROMJIAM, cover, 1, farbled, 9, Fiona Ayerst, 13, Kaygorodov Yuriy, 16–17, Kristina Vackova, 14, Richard Whitcombe, 15, Stubblefield Photography, 4, Wiroj Lee, 29; Thinkstock: Jupiterimages, 22–23, Maltaguy1, 18–19; Visuals Unlimited: Alex Kerstitch, 26–27; Wikipedia: NOAA, 12

Design Elements
Shutterstock: Gordan, Osvath Zsolt

Printed in the United States of America in Stevens Point, Wisconsin.
032014   008092WZF14

TABLE OF CONTENTS

PLENTY OF FISH IN THE SEA

Water covers 70 percent of Earth's surface. And it is crowded with life! The oceans alone provide almost 200 times as much living space as all dry land. Fish **species** make up a large part of aquatic life—more than 24,000 species. Fish are the largest group of **vertebrates** in the world. They can be found in every ocean, sea, river, and lake on the planet.

species—a group of animals with similar features
vertebrate—an animal with small bones that make up a backbone

BLUESTRIPE SNAPPER SWIM IN THE PACIFIC OCEAN. FISH ARE EVERYWHERE!

All fish share certain **adaptations**—body parts or behaviors that help them survive in their environment. Fish have gills and breathe underwater. They have fins to help them swim. Almost all have a scaly body covering. They are cold-blooded, which means the temperature inside their bodies closely matches the temperature outside. Some live in warm temperatures and others in chilly ones. All are adapted for a life spent underwater.

From rocky shores to the black depths, from warm tropics to icy polar seas, the water world is a world of extremes. And it contains some pretty amazing fish with extreme adaptations!

adaptation—a change a living thing goes through to better fit in with its environment

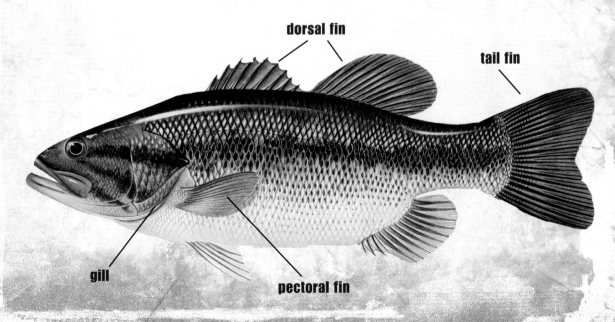

dorsal fin

tail fin

gill

pectoral fin

CHAPTER ONE

JUST ADD FRESH WATER

Freshwater is water that has no salt. The oceans contain only salt water, while most lakes and rivers are freshwater. Freshwater makes up only 2.5 percent of the world's water. But it contains more than 41 percent of all fish species. And these fish have made some amazing adaptations.

LEAPING CATFISH!

In the River Tarn in southwestern France, the European catfish hunts for birds. It can lunge out of the water and grab an unlucky pigeon standing at the edge.

Why this daring hunting behavior? Scientists don't know for sure. But this particular catfish is not **native** to the River Tarn. It's an **invasive** species, introduced in 1983. This catfish may have eaten so many native fishes that it had to find a new food source.

native—growing or living naturally in a particular place
invasive—a plant or animal that has been artificially introduced into an ecosystem

THE JAWS OF A CATFISH CAN CATCH MOST FISH—AND EVEN BIRDS OUT OF WATER.

SCALY SHARPSHOOTERS

Archerfish are found in Southeast Asia and Northern Australia. They live in a mixture of fresh and salty waters in swamps and marshes. These fish shoot water "bullets" to catch food. When they spot bugs perched on overhanging branches, archerfish take aim, spit a water bullet, and knock the bug into the water. This expert marksman can hit a target about 5 feet (1.5 meters) away.

THE ARCHERFISH SPITS A WATER BULLET AT A SPIDER. DINNER AT LAST!

FACT

Some species of archerfish can shoot only one hefty water bullet. Other species can shoot a chain of bullets rapidly, like a machine gun.

THE INCREDIBLE SAGA OF SALMON

Pacific salmon have a weird and wonderful life cycle. They begin life hatching from eggs in chilly rivers. The rivers carry the young salmon to the northern Pacific Ocean. There they grow into mature adults.

SALMON LEAPING UPSTREAM

Salmon are ready to mate between 2 and 4 years of age. At this stage they take one of the most extreme journeys of the animal kingdom. Returning to the mouth of the river they came from, the fish swim upstream. That is the only way to get back to where they hatched. Struggling to swim against the current is only part of the challenge. In spots they must hurl themselves up over rocks, rapids, and small waterfalls. Hungry bears are waiting to eat them.

Many salmon don't survive. Those that do end up in the exact spot where they were hatched. There they **spawn**, releasing eggs that settle to the riverbed. After spawning, the salmon die.

spawn—to lay eggs

LADDERS FOR SALMON

When a salmon reaches a dam, it may not make it to its spawning grounds. Many salmon die this way. Salmon ladders were invented to help salmon pass through the dams. Salmon ladders are like staircases—a series of steps. They help the salmon to leap upstairs and over the dam.

CHAPTER TWO

THE BIG BLUE

The fish of the open ocean—the ocean away from coastlines—are adapted for speed. They have streamlined bodies, strong tails, and big fins. Finding **prey** and surviving **predators** is a full-time job for open ocean dwellers. There is nowhere to hide.

A SAILFISH SHOWS OFF ITS MIGHTY DORSAL FIN.

FACT

If a sailfish feels threatened, it raises its fin as a warning. And that's not all. This excitable fish can change colors from dull brown to vivid blue and white!

FAST AND FURIOUS

Sailfish are large fish of the open ocean. They inhabit all the world's oceans except the very cold ones near the North and South Poles. Sailfish are named for their striking **dorsal fin**. It runs nearly the whole length of the fish's body. When fully extended it is much taller than the fish's height from belly to back.

Sailfish are also the fastest fish in the sea. Faster even than a cheetah on land, sailfish can swim at speeds of 68 miles (110 kilometers) per hour! This speedy fish stays safe from most predators. (Too bad, sharks!) But they are a favorite target for human anglers. When hooked, a sailfish will fight to free itself.

prey—an animal hunted by another animal for food
predator—an animal that hunts other animals for food
dorsal fin—a fin located on the back

SAILFISH ARE FAST SWIMMERS.

GOTTA FLY!

Forty species of flying fish inhabit warm waters near Earth's equator. They are medium-sized fish, no more than 18 inches (45 centimeters) long. Flying fish often make meals for many predators. But they have an extreme adaptation for getting away—they fly out of the water!

Flying fish have huge **pectoral fins** that do double duty as wings. The fish must get a good swimming start. They must beat their strong tails to reach about 37 miles (60 km) per hour. Then they rocket out of the water and flap their fins! They can keep flying above the water as far as 655 feet (200 m).

pectoral fin—one of a pair of fins found on each side of the head

FACT

Flying fish can shoot out of water as high as 4 feet (1.2 m) into the air.

A FLYING FISH GLIDES OVER THE INDIAN OCEAN.

STUCK ON YOU

Tropical ocean dwellers called remoras have adapted a neat way of being lazy. Remoras have a suction cup on their back. They attach the cup to whales, sharks, and other big, slow-moving animals, and just hang out. Not only do they get a free ride, but they get free scraps and protection too! The remora's suction cup does not hurt the host animal. And this clingy fish does offer one benefit to its host—it keeps away harmful parasites.

A REMORA LATCHES ON TO A SHARK.

CHAPTER THREE

UNDERSEA CITIES

The waters of the tropics are near the equator. Here the water is warm and calm, and there is an abundance of sea life. The tropical reef environment bustles with activity—it is like the big city of the sea. **Coral reefs** host huge populations of fish of every size and color. Competition for food is pretty stiff. But here fish also are perfectly adapted for this life.

coral reef—an underwater structure made up of the hardened bodies of corals; corals are small, colorful sea creatures

THE STONEFISH TRIES TO BLEND IN WITH ITS SURROUNDINGS.

DON'T TOUCH!

The stonefish and the lionfish are the two most **venomous** fish in the ocean. Both live in warm tropical waters. Both can deliver a sting that is powerful enough to kill a human. But they don't look the same. The stonefish is shy and disguised. Its drab and bumpy skin makes it blend in. It looks just like a rock or coral. The lionfish, on the other hand, with its striking colors and frilly fins, warns predators to keep their distance.

venomous—able to produce a poison called venom

THE LIONFISH WARNS YOU TO STAY AWAY.

WHAT'S SO FUNNY ABOUT A CLOWNFISH?

The brightly colored clownfish—or clown anemone fish—is one of the stars of the reef fishes. This tropical fish has an amazing adaptation. It safely swims among the tentacles of venomous sea anemones. Any other fish would be **paralyzed** doing that. How do they survive?

Clownfish are not immune to venom, as some think. Instead their scaly skin produces a layer of mucus that protects them from venom. Young clownfish must gradually **acclimate** to venom. They start with tiny touches of the anemone's tentacles, a little at a time. Soon the anemone no longer poses a danger, and the clownfish are right at home.

FACT

The clownfish and sea anemone benefit each other. The clownfish is safe from predators that will not go near the anemone's tentacles. In turn, the clownfish picks parasites off the sea anemone.

Clownfish rely on anemones for protection from predators. But climate change causes tiny chemical and temperature changes in the water that may be disastrous for clownfish. The changes may interfere with the clownfish's ability to detect predators, making it venture away from its safe anemone haven.

paralyze—to cause a loss of the ability to control the muscles
acclimate—to get used to something

CLOWNFISH SWIM HAPPILY AMONG THE SEA ANEMONES.

THE GENDER BENDERS

Wrasses are colorful tropical fish. More than 600 species of wrasses can be found in warm waters of the Pacific Ocean and other warm seas. Most wrasses are small, 8 inches (20 cm) or less. The largest, the humphead wrasse, can grow as big as 8 feet (2.4 m).

Wrasses live in breeding groups with one male and several females. However, if the male dies, one of the females can change into a male! How do they do this? All wrasses are born female with the ability to become male. Females can "switch on" the male parts if they need to.

EXTREME HUNTER

One wrasse in particular has an extreme hunting style. The sling-jaw wrasse can extend its mouth into a long tube measuring half the length of its body! In the blink of an eye, the fish thrusts out its vacuum-like jaws to snatch a bit of prey.

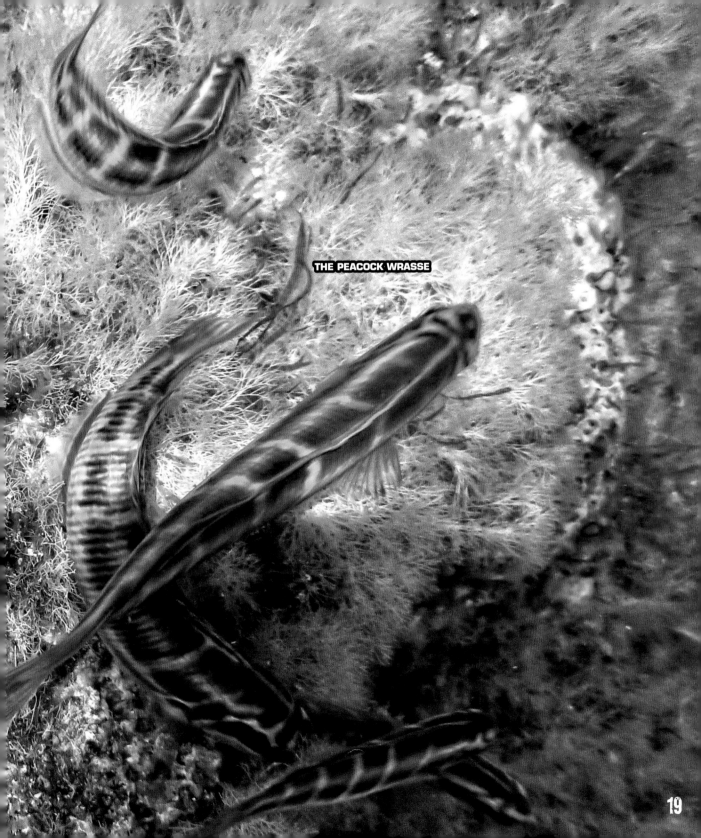

THE PEACOCK WRASSE

CHAPTER FOUR

GOING DEEPER

A mile or more beneath the surface, the ocean is dark and cold. Sunlight disappears completely at 3,280 feet (1,000 m). The temperature here is barely above freezing. Finding food is a constant challenge.

No sun means no algae for small creatures to eat. Instead they live on something called "marine snow," tiny bits of dead plants and animals that drift down to the ocean floor.

The deep sea is still largely unexplored. More people have traveled into space than have ventured into the ocean's depths!

A CLOSE-UP IMAGE OF MARINE SNOW

FACT

Another challenge of the deep sea is pressure. At great depths human lungs would collapse, but many sea animals live there comfortably. These creatures are made mostly of water, which cannot be compressed. Also, they have no lungs to be crushed.

SOME LIKE IT COLD

Sharks are found in all the world's oceans in a wide variety of habitats. Most sharks prefer at least some sunlight. But the Greenland shark is not one of them. The Greenland shark, also known as the sleeper shark, inhabits the icy Arctic Ocean, more than 1 mile (1.6 km) deep. It doesn't get much colder than that!

How does the Greenland shark survive where most fish would be frozen seafood? They have a unique adaptation—a kind of antifreeze in their body tissues. It works just like the antifreeze in cars. It keeps them from freezing in subzero environments.

THE GREENLAND SHARK IN ITS ICY HOME, THE ARCTIC OCEAN

FACT

Ever heard of the sleeper shark? Few people have. Yet the sleeper shark is the largest fish in the Arctic. And it's the second largest predatory shark in the world, after the great white!

THE SIDEWAYS LIFE

Many sea creatures make the sea floor their home. They have adaptations that make them successful bottom dwellers. Often their bodies are flattened from top to bottom, helping them blend into the seascape. One group of fish—flatfish—takes a more sideways approach.

Flatfish include flounder, sole, and halibut. They start out life looking like a typical fish. But while still young they undergo a shocking **metamorphosis**. Their bodies grow flatter from side to side and rounder from top to bottom. They end up looking more like a platter than a fish. Then the eye from one side of the head moves over to the other side! Now the fish has both eyes on the same side of its head. This is the side that always faces up as it spends the rest of its life gliding sideways along the sea floor.

metamorphosis—change in body form

Most flatfish are either left-sided or right-sided. For example, all flounder are right-sided, meaning they live right side up, left side down.

SO FLAT YOU COULD EAT OFF IT! THIS FLATFISH IS A FLOUNDER.

23

THE FISHERMAN FISH

Anglerfish are small but fierce looking. These tiny monsters have spiny backs, and their wide mouths are full of sharp teeth. Anglerfish are suited to life in the deep. Female anglerfish have their own built-in fishing lures. One of the spines on their back is extra long and curves down over their face. On the end of this spine is a small glowing tip, like a tiny lightbulb. Many animals are attracted to the light. They swim too close and get gobbled up!

THE SCARY ANGLERFISH
UP CLOSE. WATCH OUT!

Male and female anglerfish also have a crazy relationship. The male is much smaller than the female. When a male is still young, he will latch on to a female with his teeth and never let go. He becomes the female's parasite as well as her mate. Eventually, the male actually becomes a permanent part of the female's body! This weird behavior is actually a brilliant adaptation. It's difficult to find food and mates in the black deep. If you can find both at once, why go anywhere else?

FACT

One female anglerfish may host as many as six males.

THE MALE ANGLERFISH LATCHES ON TO A FEMALE.

CHAPTER FIVE

FISH OUT OF WATER?

A very small number of fish are so extreme that they don't even have to be in water! These **amphibious** species can survive out of water for a short time. In fact, some of them must leave the water for one reason or another. How do they do it and why?

amphibious—able to live on land and in water

THE "GRUNION RUN" HAPPENS EACH SPRING IN SOUTHERN CALIFORNIA.

THE RUNNING OF THE GRUNION

On the shores of southern California, an amazing event unfolds in the late spring. At high tide, during a full or new moon, thousands of small silvery fish come out of the water and wiggle onto the shore. These are grunions, and they come ashore to spawn. Locals call it the "grunion run."

After spawning, the female grunion lays her eggs in the sand. Then the male and female grunions wiggle back into the water. The eggs, safely buried deep in the sand, will hatch in about nine days. After hatching, the baby grunions are washed out to the sea.

FACT

The grunion is the only fish that spawns out of the water. This keeps the eggs safe from predators, ensuring a higher survival rate for the young.

THE AMAZING AMPHIBIOUS MUDSKIPPER

Mudskippers live in a difficult habitat for fish—tidal mudflats. Their homes are always changing in wetness and temperature. Mudskippers are adapted to spend a great deal of time out of the water. They breathe through their moist skin like an amphibian. They can also hold their gills tightly shut to keep water in and mud out.

THE MUDSKIPPER WITH ITS REMARKABLE FINS

Mudskippers live in burrows that are partly underwater. There they hide away when the sun is hot. They can even walk around on the mud with their adaptable fins. They look for tiny crabs, flies, and other small organisms to eat. Very few predators disturb their peaceful, muddy homes.

Competition among male mudskippers is fierce. When two males confront each other over territory, they raise their broad dorsal fins like a warning sign. Then they come after each other with wide-open mouths to try to frighten each other away.

Mudskippers, like numerous other fishes, have unique ways of surviving in a world full of extremes. As climate changes and other factors make survival even more challenging, there's no telling what extreme fish adaptations may be discovered!

TWO MALE MUDSKIPPERS ABOUT TO FIGHT

GLOSSARY

acclimate (AK-luh-mayte)—to get used to something

adaptation (a-dap-TAY-shuhn)—a change a living thing goes through to better fit in with its environment

amphibious (am-FI-bee-uhs)—able to live both on land and in water

coral reef (KOR-uhl REEF)—an underwater structure made up of the hardened bodies of corals; corals are small, colorful sea creatures

dorsal fin (DOR-suhl FIN)—a fin located on the back

invasive (in-VEY-siv)—a plant or animal that has been artificially introduced into an ecosystem

metamorphosis (meht-uh-MOR-fuh-siss)—a change in body form

native (NAY-tuhv)—growing or living naturally in a particular place

paralyze (PAY-ruh-lize)—to cause a loss of the ability to control the muscles

pectoral fin (PEK-ter-uhl FIN)—one of a pair of fins found on each side of the head

predator (PRED-uh-tur)—an animal that hunts other animals for food

prey (PRAY)—an animal hunted by another animal for food

spawn (SPON)—to lay eggs

species (SPEE-sheez)—a group of animals with similar features

venomous (VEN-uhm-us)—able to produce a poison called venom

vertebrate (VUR-tuh-breyt)—an animal with small bones that make up a backbone

READ MORE

Hibbert, Clare. *Fish*. Really Weird Animals. Mankato, Minn.: Arcturus Publishing, 2011.

Thomas, Isabel. *Fantastic Fish*. Extreme Animals. Chicago: Raintree, 2012.

Stille, Darlene R. *The Life Cycle of Fish*. Life Cycles. Chicago: Heinemann Library, 2012.

CRITICAL THINKING USING THE COMMON CORE

1. What does the author mean when she says "Anglerfish are suited to life in the deep" (page 24)? Which details in the text helped you confirm the author's meaning? (Key Ideas and Details)

2. What does the word *pectoral* mean in this sentence: "Flying fish have huge pectoral fins that do double duty as wings" (page 12)? What text features can you use to check that you understand this word correctly? (Craft and Structure)

3. Reread the section "The Amazing Amphibious Mudskipper" on pages 28–29. Identify two key points that the author is trying to make in this section. What evidence did the author use to illustrate her thinking? List at least three facts that were used to support the ideas. Do you agree with the author's conclusions? Why or why not? (Integration of Knowledge and Ideas)

INTERNET SITES

FactHound offers a safe, fun way to find Internet sites related to this book. All of the sites on FactHound have been researched by our staff.

Here's all you do:

Visit *www.facthound.com*

Type in this code: 9781491401651

Check out projects, games, and lots more at
www.capstonekids.com

INDEX